The Money GPS
Global Economic Collapse

David Quintieri

The Money GPS: *Global Economic Collapse*
by David Quintieri

ISBN 978-0-9879241-2-4

Table Of Contents

Section 3 – Geopolitics

Section 4 – Action Steps

The Basics

The following is some basic information you need prior to getting started.

Bull/Bear Market – A bull is a rising market and bear is a falling market.

Bond – A country takes their debt, packages it into a bond, and sells it to the public.

Treasury Bills – For the purposes of this book, they are the same as bonds–government debt.

Central Bank – Institution that manages the currency and interest rates.

Federal Reserve – U.S. central bank. Generally referred to as "The Fed".

QE – Quantitative Easing. Money printing by central banks.

Bail-Out – Using taxpayer dollars to rescue corporations.

Bail-In – Using creditor and depositor assets to rescue corporations.

Derivative – A financial instrument which may contain little to no underlying assets.

Financial Crisis – The recession which officially began in December 2007 and ended in June 2009. Mainstream media refers to it as The Great Recession.

Ben Bernanke – Fed Chairman during the Financial Crisis.

Janet Yellen – The successor to Ben Bernanke.

Globalists – Individuals in very high positions of power and/or are exceptionally wealthy. For the purposes of this book, the following terms are also interchangeable. Globalist elite, technocrats, technocratic elite, ruling elite, the powers that be, authorities, the establishment.

Introduction

Let's turn our clocks back to 2009 for a moment, when the Financial Crisis was declared to be officially over, according to the mainstream media and official statistics of the U.S. government.

Those of us who didn't receive billions in bailout money and actually pay taxes know that this is definitely not true.

Unemployment has actually become a growing epidemic, wealth inequality has increased, and poverty has taken hold of millions of people in the U.S. alone.

Let's take off our blinders, dig deeper into reality and learn what we truly face. In this theatrical tragedy we are the audience, watching in awe as the climax approaches, while the actors hide behind the curtains, in anticipation of the final scene.

Unemployment

The government provides us with an "unemployment" statistic which is defined as those who have not been able to find work for less than one year.

Fraudulently, these people are literally forgotten in the official numbers reported by the BLS.

Industries are being eviscerated by new regulations and taxation forcing corporations to either close their doors entirely, or move overseas.

Employment

To have a more accurate view of the economy, we can look at the Civilian Labor Force Participation Rate statistic.

This shows that there are consistently less people employed, a visible decline in the total workforce, and the fact that this figure sunk to a level not seen in decades.

Wealth Disparity

The old cliché of "The rich get richer and the poor get poorer" is absolutely apparent right now. This schism between the affluent and everyone else widens every single day.

The middle class is disappearing, deep under the poverty line, invariably supported entirely by government handouts.

Regulations

In 1999, we saw the repeal of the Glass-Steagall Act, allowing the possibility of monstrous financial firms which wield unlimited power over both sides of Congress.

With this power, they used billions of dollars to create trillions of dollars of dangerous derivatives.

When it began to implode in 2008, Congress hastily signed a bill handing over billions of taxpayer dollars which went to CEO bonuses and to open up factories in developing nations, permanently eliminating U.S. jobs.

In 2014, they continued the trend of deregulation by repealing a section of the Dodd-Frank bill which was put in place after the Financial Crisis specifically to stop the growth of derivatives.

Poverty

Poverty has accelerated in most countries around the world.

Government-provided statistics are broken and prove the inadequacy of a sprawling cancerous bureaucracy.

Even most mainstream media outlets have documented how people who can't make ends meet are still somehow considered above the poverty line, drastically skewing the statistics.

Revolving Door

During the Financial Crisis, new layers of the criminal collusion became evident.

Countless alumni from financial firms were now lobbying their fellow members of government for billions of dollars, less regulations, and favourable taxation.

Financial Crisis Part 2

None of the problems from the Crisis were fixed and the bandages aren't doing much to stop the gunshot wounds of the hemorrhaging economy.

Part 2 could be the implosion of the quadrillions in derivatives, it could be a hyperinflationary scenario, it could even be caused by a massive war, and it certainly could be a radical change in the monetary system.

Regardless of the road we are driven down, it all ends with a cliff.

Section 1
Foundation

Financial Crisis Part 2

We've all read about the growing divide between the rich and the poor. It's so clear now that in the U.S. alone, it hasn't been this bad since the years just prior to the Great Depression.

Many have been forced into taking two or three jobs just to pay the bills.

The government is able to manipulate the unemployment numbers using special tricks unveiled in the following paragraphs.

Criminal Schemes

1. If someone has been unemployed for a year, they are wiped from the statistics. Although the government will

never mention this statistic, you can find the BLS statistic "U6" if you search online.

2. Additionally, those people who were taking on three jobs, skews the figures as well.

3. It is also not taken into consideration that graduates who are now looking for work but can't find any, will not show up on the unemployment statistics.

Outsourced Into Poverty

Historically, our nations would be able to pull ourselves out of this mess. However, significant numbers of jobs have been outsourced to developing nations in order to increase corporate profits.

In an amazing display of double-cross, during the Financial Crisis, GM received a multi-billion dollar bailout and used the money to build factories in China and Brazil.

The Fed's Big Wallet

Previously it had been easy for the U.S. to continue their debt spiral because other countries were happily eating it up like candy.

The tide has turned and the rate at which other countries have been buying has dramatically decreased.

Trying to make up for the shortfall, the Fed's balance sheet ballooned into the trillions thanks to "Helicopter" Ben Bernanke, as these schemes continue.

Civil Unrest

Not a soul in this world will be purchasing U.S. debt soon. This will leave the Fed to be the only one picking up the tab.

After a deflationary event, a massive hyperinflation will occur, leaving the public in panic as they can not afford to eat. And if history is any guide, the riots will begin.

This is a warning.

Currency Devaluation

The word "collapse" is clearly overused in the mainstream and alternative media. More importantly, it is misunderstood.

Many people think collapse immediately equals Weimar Germany, wheelbarrows full of cash, and a dictatorial leader with a little moustache. Or even burning buildings, a police state, and nuclear bombs going off.

The history of different collapses throughout time, all the way back to the first great collapse in Athens is well documented.

Most were actually very similar. With the creation of derivatives however, a never before seen collapse will occur.

Destructive Policies

In 2002, Ben Bernanke made a speech stating that the Fed would use the same policies they have in the past.

His speech even included a devaluation of the U.S. dollar by 40%.

Bernanke specifically warned the Fed will do everything they can to prevent deflation from occurring.

Either way, the only reason to hold your savings in cash is if you're are a sheep looking to be slaughtered.

History Repeats Itself

In 1971, President Nixon removed gold from the monetary system, leaving nothing but paper garbage.

This debt-based system will bring upon a future that will unleash mass poverty on our countries.

However, those who are prepared will survive the collapse.

Central Banks

Let's turn back the pages of history to Weimar Germany.

Wheelbarrows full of cash, a rapid increase in poverty after World War 1, and a leader who promised to protect the "homeland" for his people.

Based on the Fed's track record, it's pretty clear that they've looked to Weimar for advice and chosen the route of hyperinflation.

In a first-ever and very limited audit of the Fed, it was found that they had printed over $16 trillion during the Financial Crisis and gave it to foreign institutions and corporations in every corner of the world!

All other activities have never been accounted for.

Two Weapons

Remember Bernanke stated that the Fed would use every weapon in its arsenal to prevent deflation from occurring.

Although the Fed claims that they have many weapons, realistically however, they only have two: Interest rates and money printing.

The Financial Crisis allowed them to bring out weapon #1: Interest rates. They exhausted that ammunition very quickly once it hit rock bottom at 0%.

Since then, they have printed trillions of dollars and handed it out to their friends all over the world.

Hyperinflation Nation

There are many cases of hyperinflation throughout world history. In more recent history, Zimbabwe, Yugoslavia, Venezuela, and many more, completely inflated their currencies into oblivion.

Americans have experienced this multiple times before. One example is the the Continental dollar which was printed with no backing as a scheme to finance war.

Sound familiar?

Once the public stopped accepting them, the currency rapidly declined in value and the printing presses began to run at full speed. And so, the saying "Not worth a Continental" was born.

History As A Guide

The tap is now open and historically has never been able to be shut off.

A hyperinflation is the end result for any country which attempts to print their way out of debt.

Open Market Operations

Interest rates are an important indicator of the health of any economy.

After the Financial Crisis introduction of historically low rates, buying a house or getting a loan became practically free money.

Something has certainly changed because back in 1980, interest rates hit a high of 20%.

Printing Press

There are different factors which move the interest rates up or down. Today, the primary cause is courtesy of the Federal Reserve.

What is this magic wand that the government waves to

manipulate these interest rates?

It's called: Open Market Operations.

Just like a garage sale, the government will periodically make some money by selling off its old junk (Debt). The Fed goes to the garage sale and buys up everything that nobody else wants.

The magic is when you understand where the Fed gets their money from: They get it by simply adding it to their bank account. Voila!

Inflationary Policies

There are two reasons why this is the worst idea in history.

1. Despite what the government believes, you cannot create paper money out of thin air and not have it create inflation.

Just like with diamonds, the more scarce something is, the more value it is perceived to have.

Likewise, once these dollars are expanded dramatically, they no longer have the value they once had.

2. Printing money to buy debt is an entirely fictional puppet show. This cannot increase productivity, let alone pull a nation out of recession.

This can only be a scheme to fund the banks and

redistribute wealth from the middle class to the globalists.

Too Big To Fail

Whether it's a bail-out, bail-in, or any other scheme, governments around the world have shown us that paper currency is discredited.

When you hold paper dollars or even worse, digital dollars in a bank account, you are fuelling this corrupt system and giving the banksters leverage to use against us.

Inflation Or Deflation?

The Fed has pursued a policy of destroying the wealth of all Americans since its creation in 1913.

Inflation is a policy followed by every single central bank in the world.

However, a deflation could certainly happen.

Debt-Based System

A deflation occurs when people lose faith in the financial system and begin paying down their debt, stop borrowing, and don't spend their savings.

Our fiat monetary system is based on debt and is designed to continuously increase. When the trend begins to reverse, a deflation is setting in.

Weimar Germany

If we look throughout history, we'll see that governments are simply making the same mistakes over and over again. The result of which is relatively predictable.

In *Guide to Investing in Gold and Silver*, Mike Maloney predicts that the U.S. will enter a state of significant deflation.

At this point, they will fire up the printing presses, causing a hyperinflation.

In Weimar Germany, the Reichbank was printing quadrillions of Marks every day! That's the magnitude of hyperinflation the Fed is racing towards.

Up Or Down?

Based on historical data, it won't be a case of inflation or deflation. It will most likely be one after the other.

The deflation won't last very long before it rapidly changes into inflation.

Food stamp usage will break records as well as other social assistance programs.

In a not-so-shocking coincidence, the deflation will allow the globalists to pick up stocks and other investments at rock-bottom prices.

Victims Of Tyranny

In the end, the currency will be destroyed.

The general public who held onto paper dollars will be victim to a takeover of the financial system by the ruling elite.

Don't be a victim.

Interest Rates

You may remember that in 1980, interest rates peaked out at 20% in a desperate attempt to calm down rapidly advancing inflation.

In reference to the post-Financial Crisis mess, Alan Greenspan stated that in order to keep inflation rates below two per cent, "the Fed...would have to constrain monetary expansion so drastically that it could temporarily drive up interest rates into the double-digit range."

The fact which bankers and analysts will not discuss is that if interest rates make their way up to even half of what they were a few decades ago, mass foreclosures would invariably occur worldwide.

Not to mention the fact that a small increase in interest rates would make the national debt unserviceable.

Negative Return

After the Financial Crisis, interest rates were pushed down to historic lows in a desperate effort to keep currency flowing.

Germany, widely viewed as the strongest EU member, began selling Treasury Bills with a negative yield because it was still seen as a "safe" investment.

The truth is that safety is an illusion in any market because of the clear and evident fraud and corruption.

Banker Theft

There are many levels of theft in the financial system but let's focus on the next level of criminality created by bankers: Negative interest rates.

In 2010, Janet Yellen stated that "If it were positive to take interest rates into negative territory I would be voting for that."

Some central banks such as Japan, Switzerland, Sweden, and Denmark have imposed negative interest rates, leaving investors with fewer options and a grim outlook on the future of their money.

The Next Crash

Managing our money is a constant battle because we've

watched our savings slowly deteriorate by the process of inflation.

With interest rates at rock bottom and an economy continuing to slide, negative interest rates may become a standard policy once faced with crisis.

Now with the threat of bail-in's as well as negative rates, we're running out of places to hide.

Manipulation

Interest rates aren't decided by the market and certainly aren't where they should be.

As discussed in a previous chapter, Open Market Operations keep these rates low and it looks like central banks are willing take this even lower, should they deem it necessary.

If your money is in the banking system, you will be caught in the crosshairs of the schemes of the globalists.

Don't be sold by the propaganda while they rob you blind.

Reserve Currency

There has been a massive geopolitical shift which has not been felt since World War 2.

In recent decades, financial markets as well as governments have generally accounted for the U.S. dollar to be the safe haven of the world—unshakable, unbreakable.

Reserve Status

A reserve currency is used to promote stability in trade between countries simply because its purpose is to be strong and secure over long periods of time.

International trade generally takes place using a reserve currency which means converting their own currencies before the exchange.

This equates to transaction costs, making trade more expensive.

In addition, all commodities are priced in the reserve currency. This is important to know because the price of a commodity is linked not only its value but the exchange rate between the buyers' currency and the reserve currency.

China

Countless countries throughout the world now have currency swap agreements with China which continue to be renewed and expanded.

From South American countries like Brazil and Argentina, to African countries like Ghana and Zimbabwe, to the EU, Australia, New Zealand, and Canada, all of which now do a portion of their trade with China in yuan instead of dollars.

The U.S. dollar will slowly fade away as the reserve currency of the world, nations will buy less U.S. debt, causing the Fed to step in and pick up the slack.

Crystal Ball

Many economists are awaiting a spark which will generate a collapse, causing disorder on global currencies.

Instead, the more likely scenario is that this will decay in a slow and gradual cancerous death for the U.S. dollar.

This of course assumes the world continues on its current trajectory and we aren't exposed to a true Black Swan event.

An event no economist or banker could predict.

Taxes

Despite the media's effort to hide it, several cities have rumbled with mass civil unrest. That chaos has a domino effect which will spread to most major cities around the world.

Instability could be generated by the possibility of hyperinflation or deflation as previously discussed, but we could also experience massive taxation.

Monetary Slavery

Historically, serfs would be forced to pay about a 10% tax rate. Any higher and they would revolt. Today only the big corporations can get away with paying such a low rate.

In recent times, France attempted to tax thousands of wealthy individuals from 75% to as much as 100%! This shouldn't be considered taxation, it should be considered absolute theft.

Death And Taxes

In the U.S., income tax was signed into law in 1913. Without coincidence, the same year as the introduction of the Federal Reserve.

Today, it's practically blasphemy to suggest not paying into our own slavery. Still, income and property taxes were not enough to satisfy the gluttony of a big government.

In many countries around the world, a Value Added Tax was introduced. A VAT for citizens to pay their "fair share".

Green Scheme

The most recent leech on the people has been the introduction of carbon taxes.

Under the guise of stopping "climate change", some governments have decided to tax any industry that outputs carbon dioxide and greenhouse gases.

At the same time giving waivers to companies like GE so that they can maintain a 0% tax rate.

Of course, the businesses simply pass their increased overhead onto the customer, equating to higher prices, environmental fees, and other hidden taxes.

It seems as though governments around the world have been engaging in theft, backed by the law under a scheme known as taxation.

Taxation is a totalitarian system of control and they are using it as a weapon against us.

Austerity

Power is being transferred into the hands of the few.

The IMF is a supranational entity that is made up of nearly 200 countries and was created just after World War 2.

The IMF is a UN agency and could perhaps be seen as their financial goon squad.

IMF Power

After reading countless whitepapers of the globalists while researching for *The Money GPS*, I was able to predict that:

"The IMF will become more powerful as the Crisis worsens." (68).

"Additional international organizations or funds will be

created and existing ones will have their powers expanded."
(245).

On April 19th, 2012, the Wall Street Journal reported
Christine Lagarde stating increased funding for the IMF.

Vultures Picnic

After Greece began getting torn apart by the financial
vultures, they needed to sell off precious assets in order to
make back their money.

As an example, in 2013, the Emir of Qatar bought six
Greek islands for rock-bottom prices.

Since then, Greece has been forced to engage in an
expanded privatization program to help pay off the banker-
created debt.

It's only a matter of time before priceless national treasures
like the Coliseum and the Eiffel Tower get sold off to the
banking establishments and major corporations.

IMF Playbook

Former World Bank chief economist Joseph Stiglitz
revealed detailed information about the IMF and their
criminality.

He explained that a country takes on too much debt and
eventually finds itself near default. They will publicly state

that they require funding.

The IMF steps in and loans a portion of your tax dollars to that country on absurd terms to this desperate country. The country cannot pay it back because of the austerity imposed on them so it is forced to sell off its assets.

A process that is a broken record, playing over and over again all around the world.

When you are told the IMF is coming to your aid, your time has come.

Credit Unions

Since the introduction of central banking, the value of our currencies have been declining in relation to our incomes, leaving individuals increasingly more destitute, every day.

The majority of people unknowingly leave their cash in the banks as a form of savings, with the thought that it will be there when they need to take it out.

Historically there have been countless events of bank runs in which the unsuspecting citizens encounter a rush to empty out their accounts in search of safety.

David vs. Goliath

Massive banks often use derivatives to gamble in this fiat system while risking their clients' money, knowing that there will always be a bailout for them.

With deposit insurance in place to protect the savers, people no longer worry about the threat of losing their savings.

Seeking Shelter

On a theoretical level, credit unions could be safer than a big bank and offer more stability.

It may not fluctuate wildly like some of these banks with all of their gambling and derivatives.

They're not as widely recognized as the big banks which may limit your ability to transact using them, so keep this in mind.

Underlying Issues

It is crucial to understand that they are still dealing with the same fiat currency. It is the currency which is being devalued every single day, thanks to central banking. Inflation will eat away at it far beyond the interest gained on the account.

Another issue is the bail-in's which are essentially a way to scoop money out of bank accounts to recapitalize the institution.

The bankers and governments may promise that your money is safe but it would be foolish to believe anything these technocrats and politicians say.

Debt

Ultimately those in debt will suffer most. That seems the most likely scenario. Get out of any debt first before this crash and you will always do better than others.

Debt is the system created by the globalists in order to enslave humanity. Defund their operation.

Section 2
Crisis

Collusion

You've seen this in every country around the world. Sometimes governments will do it, sometimes the central banks, and sometimes an international organization.

Bailouts.

In 2008, the U.S. government began bailing out many of their industries, particularly in the financial sector, to prevent the ship from sinking.

Bailouts

Many countries have decided to bailout their financial firms as the contagion spread like a disease.

The theory of a bailout is that money can be redistributed from the taxpayer to the sector or corporations in need.

A perfect display of socialism.

Trillions of dollars have been handed out to banks all around the world. Then almost instantly, that money was evaporated by the criminals in collusion with government.

It is with absolute certainty through documented fact that bailouts serve absolutely no benefit to the public.

Bailouts claim to help the banks by protecting our deposits. However, these "banks" are often just corporations that take super risky bets and then when it turns sour, they'll run crying to their alumni in government positions for money.

Financial Tyranny

The Financial Crisis that became clearly visible in 2008, was not a "Too Big to Fail" situation. It was designed specifically to hand out taxpayer money to particular institutions.

Governments are used as a tool for corporations and globalists to manipulate.

The following are just a couple examples of this treason.

Leading up to the Financial Crisis, former CEO of Goldman Sachs, Henry Paulson became Treasury Secretary and gave himself a $200 million tax break.

Then, the U.S. government created a stimulus package

funded by taxpayers known as TARP.

Congressman Brad Sherman stated on the floor of the House "Many of us were told in private conversations that if we voted against this bill on Monday that the sky would fall, the market would drop two or three thousand points the first day, another couple of thousand the second day, and a few members were even told that there would be martial law in America if we voted no."

That's called terrorism.

Crutch Or Collapse

Bailouts have become more common over the years and will continue to escalate and expand.

A bailout is a crutch. If the crutch is pulled out, the system will collapse.

Printing Money

During the Financial Crisis in 2008, subprime mortgages were failing and the panic in the media finally emerged. This was followed by a Viral Contagion, taking everything with it.

Unprecedented bailouts were the response from the U.S. government (And most others around the world).

Trillions were handed out to corporations and it barely kept the global financial system alive.

After two failed rounds of monetary easing from the Fed, many economists, portfolio managers, and others in the financial field were begging and pleading for a third round of money printing.

Their jobs certainly depended on it.

Devaluation

The Fed and countless others in government insisted that there would not be a QE3.

Former Fed chairman Alan Greenspan had stated that he would have been surprised if there was a QE3 because it would "continue erosion of the dollar."

Since QE3 was unequivocally just a matter of time, it was boldly mentioned in *The Money GPS*:

"Round 3 of money printing is inevitable." (238).

On September 12, 2012, the Fed officially introduced QE3.

Crystal Ball

The U.S. is following in the footsteps of Weimar Germany, Venezuela, and Zimbabwe.

It doesn't require a crystal ball to figure out where the U.S. dollar is headed. It does however require the ability to reject the mainstream media and their propaganda.

Before the currency is devalued under hyperinflation, the banks will initiate capital controls and bank holidays to prevent bank runs.

Then, the earth will rumble under the heels of the angry mobs.

Bailouts

If the Financial Crisis has taught us anything, it's that the easiest way to make money is to become a banker and receive billions of dollars in a taxpayer-funded bailout scheme.

Historically, a bank would hold onto your money (Precious metals) and give you a paper note to make your daily purchases easier to manage.

With the introduction of fractional reserve banking, the bankers were able to loan out many more notes than precious metals in their vaults.

Escalating corporate greed required them to have ever-increasing profits and so, riskier and riskier bets were placed, without concern for the inevitable failure.

The Bailout Game

Bailouts have been a strategy for governments to collude with the bankers in order to hand out trillions in taxpayer money directly to the financial institutions.

As the Financial Crisis began to spread, we watched the criminality of financial fraud as cracks began to show.

In *The Money GPS*, there is a specific prediction that Greece would require not just two bailouts, but they would require even more.

"A second round of bailouts for Greece is needed. Despite the billions given during the first round, it just wasn't enough. It will continue." (68).

IMF Bloodshed

Once the IMF has negotiated a deal with a government, the bailouts are designed to never cease. Intentional and deliberately unfair terms are part of the loan which can realistically never be paid back.

This is like trying to swim with a ball and chain attached to your ankle.

Failed Policies

The truth is that bailouts must continue in order to keep this system afloat.

However, the goal of these bailouts are not to prop up the system. They are to redistribute wealth from the middle class to the globalists.

The real economy is long gone. All that's left is the fairy tale of stimulus packages and easy money.

In the end, all currencies will be destroyed in a domino effect, transferring the wealth to those holding real assets.

Viral Contagion

The world is under a system of globalization which has been promoted as the reason for economic growth of the past few decades.

The thought is that as long as the Fed continues to print money, China keeps buying trillions in U.S. debt, and the U.S. military continues to expand its empire, the financial system will continue to perform well.

The Virus

But what about when times get tough?

This system is so interconnected and intertwined that a problem in one country becomes a problem everywhere else (With varying degrees of magnitude).

During the massive political upheaval which occurred in Greece, the Crisis clearly exposed the rotting core of the EU.

The Money GPS explicitly predicted that the Euro Viral Contagion would continue to spread into Spain and Italy.

"Ireland, Greece, and Portugal have all received bailouts to keep their economies afloat. The eyes are now on Spain and Italy as the cracks have began to show in their markets as well." (4).

"There is contagion in the system; therefore, we can expect more bailouts to occur." (68).

Inevitably, the ECB began buying bonds of countries including Spain and Italy to prevent a complete collapse.

Global Governance

Each bailout discussion and every meeting of supranational entities like the G20, IMF, or the EU, in every case brings upon what countless high-level officials have publicly referred to as "Global Governance".

This tyranny has been marketed as a way to keep watch on each other to ensure nations aren't breaking the rules (Created by unelected technocrats).

With globalization fully intact, the globalists can manipulate and cause a crisis in one country knowing how the ripple effect will ultimately occur.

U.S. Dollar Collapse

Many foolish and shortsighted people outside of the U.S. have not only been complacent about the collapse of America but have encouraged it.

During the Financial Crisis, the whole system began to tumble all around the world once the subprime mortgages fell apart. This is a perfect example of an American problem becoming a global problem.

The Viral Contagion isn't over. It's heading to your doorstep.

New Monetary System

After World War 2, all of the gold from Europe began flowing into the U.S., creating a rock solid foundation for investment.

In 1944, the Bretton Woods agreement was formed, giving the U.S. the reserve currency status and therefore, a monopoly.   All goods and services traded between countries had to be exchanged into U.S. dollars first.

Despite this, the U.S. has fallen victim to financial turmoil, massive debt, and a declining jobs market.

War Is On

The shift of power from the U.S. to the emerging markets has already begun taking place.

Dozens of countries have formed agreements with others to stop using the dollar and begin using their own currencies to do trade.

The monopoly is threatened. And so, the currency war is on.

Hegelian Dialectic

Supranational entities like the IMF may attempt to provide a solution to the coming crisis. They already have their fiat digital currency which is used when bailing out countries: The SDR.

This may be the globalists opportunity to introduce the SDR (Or another currency) as the global reserve currency.

In doing so, the monopoly that the U.S. has will be handed over to a group of unelected, unaccountable technocrats.

The tyranny of the globalists will be magnified dramatically if this is allowed to occur.

Those who have their savings in paper assets could be wiped out.

Money Is Finite

Everything has a lifespan and currencies are no exception to this rule, despite what we have been led to believe.

It has been calculated that approximately every 30-40 years a new monetary system emerges. We have seen the Classical Gold Standard, Gold Exchange Standard, and more recently, the Dollar Standard, in addition to others throughout history.

We are certainly overdue.

The New Monetary System

As Rahm Emmanuel stated "Never let a crisis go to waste."

Today we have an expansion of debt on every single level possible, including: National, corporate, and household.

Since all countries allow central bank control over their money supply, this formulates a policy of ever-expanding debt.

Central banks print money out of thin air and lend it to commercial banks at interest, who then lend it to you at much higher rates.

This is a system of perpetual and continual debt because in order to pay off the debt, more money needs to be created!

Derivatives Nightmare

Financial institutions engage in gambling whereby they literally create an "asset" which may not even be real.

Derivatives are a part of this mess when in many situations there may be no underlying asset at all.

The derivatives will be used to hold us hostage and that day is drawing near.

The New Paradigm

Supranational entities such as the IMF are ready to take advantage of a dying system, pose as the saviours by introducing a new currency to back our present ones, allowing their friends and counterparts to attain the maximum level of control over the monetary system.

Whether it's the derivatives which insider Warren Buffet referred to as "financial weapons of mass destruction", or a potential massive stock market crash, a global bail-in, a painful revaluation of retirement accounts, or the much talked about entitlement reforms and their obvious backlash, a new paradigm will be encountered.

Once the trigger is pulled, it will be far too late for you to react.

High Frequency Trading

The Financial Crisis exposed the underlying fraud that was shockingly determined to be legal.

There are many systems available to the bankers to create ever-increasing profits and High Frequency Trading (HFT) is just one of them.

HFT uses very expensive high speed networks combined with computer algorithms to automatically trade stocks.

In fact, most stocks are now traded by computer programs, requiring no human intervention.

HFT works so fast that it is able to see that you want to buy a stock, it can then sneak ahead of you, buy it, then sell it to you at a higher price.

Monopoly Men

This idea that companies that can afford a system which undermines the individual is simply a monopoly.

The danger is that the bankers are able to manipulate the stock markets at a rapid pace. They could cause a spike in a stock or could easily cause a crash and buy up everything after other investors sell.

Flash Crash

In 2010, there was a Flash Crash that occurred which resulted in a 1000-point drop in the Dow in a single day— Its biggest drop ever.

This was a direct result of HFT gone wrong, where triggers in the algorithms set off automatic selling and panicked the market.

This flash should have been a warning signal to all investors about the fragility of the market and where their retirement savings are sitting.

Risk vs. Reward

Our retirement accounts, pension funds, and even the well-being of corporations, depend on the stability of the financial markets.

HFT is a disaster waiting to happen, that's for certain.

The issue that may plague us at some point is, what if this is used as a tool to intentionally cause a crash in order to profit from it?

Where there is risk, there will be failure.

The Crash Ahead

If you want to preserve your wealth at this time, you have one option and that is to take your money out of paper investments and hold your savings in assets that are real.

It's a fact that there will be companies and stocks which survive even the biggest crashes, perhaps continuing to pay dividends as well. The challenge presents itself with managing risk.

Will the stock you have chosen be one which survives or one that evaporates into dust?

When choosing to preserve your wealth, choose with caution, patience, and knowledge.

Bail-In's & Capital Controls

When a stock market rises, investors rush in to ride this wave not knowing where it came from. The Fed generates this wave with its printing press, fueling an infinite rise.

This artificial stimulation comes at a price which will not be seen right away, so they can get away without taking any blame.

John Maynard Keynes once said: "By a continuing process of inflation, governments can confiscate, secretly and unobserved, an important part of the wealth of their citizens."

Control And Profit

Paper assets are the only option for individuals because financial advisors will never recommend anything else.

They make commission based on selling particular products. So by recommending that you purchase gold and silver bullion for example, they won't be able to profit from it.

Paper currency allows an oligarchy to silently rule over the monetary system and ensure the currency flows into their hands with special laws created for them by their insiders in government.

Cashless Society

The governments introduce new laws and the banks introduce new regulations, in order to progress in stages towards a cashless society.

Paper currency (Despite its flaws) can be stored in one's personal possession and can also be traded between two people without the knowledge of a third party.

A bail-in is an obvious threat to a saver because any currency in the banks can easily be stolen without warning.

Additionally, a bank holiday is also dangerous because you would no longer have access to your money to buy necessities such as food.

Also, governments can repeat history and could revalue the currency overnight, instantly destroying a part of your wealth. A policy which has been implemented several times throughout history.

Paper Profits

You can ride the wave of great profits in the paper markets as many surely have.

Since the game is rigged and all figures and documentation prove a manipulation, why risk your savings to a system that was publicly built and designed by a small group of bankers, specifically with the purpose of having maximum control and profit?

The sheep who blindly hand over their savings will certainly lose it.

Precious Metals

What is your favourite asset?

Even for those who are certain precious metals are a real asset worth adding to their portfolio, there is still much argument over which is "better" and the percentage of each to hold.

Precious metals are an excellent investment which have proven to hold value through generations and should be included as part of an extremely well-diversified portfolio of real assets. The more diversified the portfolio, the more safety and security it will provide you during times of bear markets.

The following are the absolute facts and is left up to you to decide which direction you will go.

The Real Facts

Historically, gold and silver have been money, have held value for thousands of years, and have never gone bankrupt (Unlike countless companies and countries).

In many cases, gold and silver mines open when prices exceed the cost of getting them out of the ground. Likewise, they will close when it's just not worth it.

Silver differs from gold in that it is often mined as a byproduct of other metals.

Recent figures show that comparatively, silver is consumed at a much higher rate than gold which will ultimately bring about a supply issue even if investment demand decreases.

When owning precious metals, you are purchasing an insurance policy as well as betting that the value of paper dollars will decline.

The question is, which should you buy?

Gold Or Silver?

The short answer: Own both!

Both silver and gold have their own positive and negative aspects but will ultimately have value when the next monetary system is forced upon us.

Gold

Once the Financial Crisis hit, some central banks began purchasing gold at a rate of thousands of tonnes per year.

Gold is widely viewed as the greatest hedge against inflation and also seen as a bet against the U.S. dollar.

In terms of its price, gold tends to be more stable than silver which for example in 2008 went from $21 to $9 within just a few months.

In many cultures, gold is purchased as a means of storing wealth through generations (A tradition not practiced in most Western countries).

This is most evident in China and India.

Silver

There is a direct proportional relationship between the increase in technology in our daily lives and the amount of silver being used as a commodity.

Silver is widely consumed in products such as electronics, solar panels, batteries, photography, jewelry, silverware, bearings, brazing and soldering, dental amalgam, mirrors, and water purification.

Silver tends to lag behind gold in its bull market, so when investors believe that gold has become too expensive, many rush in on silver causing a huge spike in its price.

Preserving Your Wealth

Remember that nothing is bulletproof and you shouldn't put all of your savings into any one asset, including gold and silver, despite the fact that it is a great way to preserve wealth during hard times.

The Money GPS Strategy is all about diversification even within the asset class itself, which is unlike most money managers who consider an all-paper portfolio to be "diversified".

Coins, bars, and "junk" silver are the most obvious and most important part of the precious metals portion of a portfolio.

Buy whatever you can afford, a small amount at a time, and buy in small denominations as well. For example, instead of buying just one type of coin, you could diversify and buy Gold Eagles, Maple Leafs, and Krugerrand's.

For some individuals, silverware, collectables, and even high-carat jewelry are a great balance between an investment and enjoyment.

Paper Will Fall

Precious metals are essential because they hold value through generations, unlike garbage paper currency.

Whichever you choose, it doesn't matter as long as you're getting out of fiat and into real assets.

Debt-Based Monetary System

Since the introduction of central banking, governments have signed onto a system of perpetual debt.

Once again, a central bank creates money out of thin air, loans it to commercial banks at interest, who then loan it to you at a much higher rate of interest.

This scheme is an absolute monopoly because the central bank's currency is the only legal option.

Debt-Based System

Governments must always dig themselves deeper into debt because it would collapse the monetary system otherwise.

No longer is there real value and a surplus, there is only more and more debt.

It is a fact that the most powerful and influential nations are those who are most indebted.

Debt is the new wealth.

Government Sponsored Profit

When you look at the historical data, the more control the globalists have over the banking system, you will notice a growing income inequality between the rich and the poor.

In 1933, the Glass-Steagall Act was implemented in order to prevent investment institutions from getting too big by requiring them to be separate from banks.

It was repealed in 1999, setting off a major boom in the corporate profits of these corporations.

Multinational corporations have been legally allowed to increase their wealth created from thin air using all sorts of garbage financial "instruments".

Debt Instrument

Let's take the example of a Collateralized Debt Obligation. A C.D.O. is literally an instrument of debt.

These corporations had the brilliant idea of taking all sorts of bad debt such as car loans, mortgages, and credit card debt, package it up, put a nice little bow on top, and call it a "C.D.O."

To top it all off, they got their friends at the rating agencies to give them a AAA rating—the highest rating possible.

Pay Off Your Debt

It was disclosed post-Financial Crisis years that your mortgage may have actually been sold off to a third party and has been used in all sorts of high risk gambling instruments of debt.

When you pay off your debt, you are fighting against the bankers by defunding them.

Additionally, eliminating debt allows you the security in an uncertain future of the threat of rising interest rates.

So it's crucial that you remove all debt, take your savings and invest in your assets, and work diligently to lessen your dependence on a system that is constantly finding ways to steal your wealth and keep you down.

Wealth Confiscation

There will be a great upheaval when this monetary system fails and a new one takes its place.

The general public believes that a pension fund is a guaranteed payout which they can live on once they retire.

Unfortunately for these people, the sun will set on this false ideology when criminal schemes of the bankers take full effect.

Currently in the U.S., the majority of its pension funds invest in stocks, Treasury Bills, and are increasing their positions in newly created financial instruments.

If the financial markets take a nosedive, so will the value of these pension funds.

Alphabet Soup Of Trash

Particularly since the 1980's, an *Infectious Greed* has run through the system, engaging in financial misconduct with the creation and now abundance of garbage such as C.D.O's, C.D.S's, M.B.S's, and the rest of the alphabet.

Using these tools, bankers have swindled politicians into putting their city and state's investments in these newly created black holes.

The money in pension funds are riding on the fact that the stock market will continue its perpetual boom, ignoring the reality of this situation.

Theft By Government

There have been examples of pension funds being looted in recent history, which are just the first of many more to come in a global confiscation of wealth. Pension theft has occurred in New Jersey, Ireland, Canada, France, and more.

In Detroit, pension funds were cut as a result of the city gone bankrupt.

Poland confiscated half of private pension funds in order to reduce the debt of the nation.

In Portugal they did the same, using private assets to cover up public mistakes.

Unfolding Events

As we saw during the Financial Crisis, when a stock market crashes, it isn't just an isolated event.

All markets are interconnected globally, so when companies stop hiring and begin laying off employees, it causes these individuals to purchase less, hindering the economy.

Retirement accounts have systematically been stolen by greedy bankers and the general public is unaware how it works.

Even Social Security which is life support for many, is a complete fraud that will have to one day be "reformed", massively increasing poverty.

Economist Richard Duncan stated "Social Security is an unfunded pension scheme" and it is the undeniable truth.

Preservation Of Wealth

Unfortunately, just like most mortgages, retirement accounts are the property of the same bankers who lobby the government to impose more taxes on you and more bailouts for them.

People need to change their idea of money altogether, reduce their dependence on the system, and benefit from the safety and security of *The Money GPS Strategy*.

Section 3
Geopolitics

The Globalists

History has proven that absolute power corrupts absolutely. When given the chance to consume power, any nation, organization, or institution will exceed the boundaries of their designated scope.

Governments are overrun by the alumni of major corporations. In other cases, they are simply bribed through legal means using lobbyists.

Using government as a tool, the globalists can impose their will upon the public, silently.

Let's look at some of the institutions and entities which have been created, claiming the intention of security, prosperity, or stability, and then connect the dots as to what the actual results have been.

United Nations

World War 1 introduced global unification with the establishment of The League of Nations. This was replaced by the United Nations in 1945.

"Due to the powers vested in its Charter and its unique international character, the United Nations can take action on the issues confronting humanity in the 21st century, such as peace and security, climate change, sustainable development, human rights, disarmament, terrorism, humanitarian and health emergencies, gender equality, governance, food production, and more."

Ultimately, the UN creates treaties which are not legally binding anywhere in the world since this supranational cabal is not part of elected governments. Representatives, or more accurately, lobbyists, attempt to push these through their respective Congress/Parliament to create laws, constructing global uniform policies.

UN Agenda 21 is a prime example of a global governance, pushed through governments at the local level in countries all around the world.

NATO

NATO follows a similar path, having its roots in a time just after World War 2. Its mission is to form a global army which aims to protect the collective and standardize plans put out by the Military Industrial Complex.

In 2012, the power of this group became evident of when U.S. Defense Secretary Leon Panetta told Senator Jeff Sessions that they would not seek congressional approval to go to war: "Our goal would be to seek international permission and come to the Congress and inform you. Whether or not we would want to get permission from the Congress, those are issues we would have to discuss."

A treasonous act committed in the face of the elected representatives and not a single person was reprimanded.

European Union

The EU began post-World War 2 as well, this time with economic and political agreements of the coal and steel industries.

The introduction of the Euro bound and shackled several countries to the common interest rate and currency. A single group of unelected technocrats rule from overhead, creating laws for the countries which reside within the autocratic EU.

A common central bank is used to dictate monetary policy which has clearly been an absolute failure.

International Monetary Fund

According to their official website "Created in 1945, the IMF is governed by and accountable to the 188 countries that make up its near-global membership."

Their accountability however, has clearly shown the member nations don't actually have influence in IMF actions. This is yet another group of unelected globalists, squeezing the life out of weaker nations. Their activities indicate that the terms of their bailout agreements are intended to strangle a nation purposely in order to force it to sell off their most precious assets.

This has been documented most recently in Greece.

Dictatorship

A dictator gets into power by using fear. Scare the public into anxiously accepting their own slavery in order to protect them. From Hitler's 1933 law known as the Enabling Act, to the Obama masterpiece, the NDAA, dictators always find a way to have a legal basis for their actions.

The NDAA is written with language so vague that the President can indefinitely detain and murder U.S. citizens should they be under suspicion of terrorist activity.

This is known as a dictator.

Democide

In its viral spread, once a cancer overtakes the host, that person dies, taking the cancer with it. In terms of our governments, they suck the citizens dry until there is simply nothing left to take.

This is democide: Death by government.

Accurate estimates from the University of Hawaii indicate a completely shocking statistic that over 260 million people were murdered by their own government in the 20th century alone.

Truth

All of these institutions created false promises of prosperity, security, and even world peace. Once fully integrated, it became obvious that this was done at the expense of sovereignty. Their stated goals were never met, yet the losses are still putting a heavy burden upon humanity.

We must fight for individual sovereignty. We must use our right of free speech or it will be taken away. We must always speak our minds and seek the truth.

Democracy

A wise man once said that democracy is two wolves and a sheep voting on what's for dinner.

It's quite obvious what's for dinner!

The present system of government in many nations is supposed to be one of democracy. But in no way, shape, or form does the voice of the people actually get heard.

In times of outrage, the public turns to the ballot box. They believe that by voting for their only other option (The other party), they will get the results they want. Of course this isn't true because the government structure is a duopoly. Like a snake with two heads.

Politicians must ultimately obey the commands of those who bankroll and control them.

Bribes Are Legal

Major corporations and industries lobby (Bribe) government bureaucrats in order to have laws passed in their favour.

The biotech industry is a prime example, having their alumni working in every corner of government in all relevant sectors.

Big biotech lobbyists managed to have the U.S. government pass the Plant Protection Act. This law literally grants biotech corporations immunity. No matter how deadly their poisonous creations are, they can't be held accountable in court.

The political system is specifically designed to keep wealth and power within the inner circle.

Money Buys Power

It takes a considerable amount of money to run as a political leader. The higher up the ladder, the more money it will take to get exposure in the media.

Leading up to the 2008 elections, Obama received nearly a billion dollars in campaign funding, primarily from financial institutions.

Shortly after being elected, those institutions received multi-billion dollar bailouts and regulations in their favour.

Grassroots

This system masquerades as democratic and that a new leader can make change. The truth however, isn't a fairy tale.

We must acknowledge the failure of government. Real change must come from the grassroots.

Lessen your dependence on the government by increasing your knowledge and applying *The Money GPS Strategy*.

War

Now more than ever before, the threat of World War 3 looms over humanity as the vast majority remain clueless to the possibility.

Political tension thickens as countries begin forming new alliances which break down others previously set in stone.

In a short period of time, war has evolved from direct combat in the trenches to the disconnected battle of drone warfare. As technology has become more pervasive, a new era of war has emerged.

The following is a brief overview of what we could face.

Thermonuclear War

It isn't science fiction to assume nukes may fall from the

skies, creating havoc as they scorch the earth.

In 1945, during World War 2, we witnessed the U.S. murdering hundreds of thousands of Japanese in Hiroshima and Nagasaki.

Since then, thousands of nuclear weapons have been detonated during testing, many of them in the Nevada desert.

China, Russia, and the U.S. have made their operations public that they are preparing for nuclear war.

Currency War

In a hot war, enemies are distinct and their effects are visible. A currency war is much more deceptive because it can be done through the financial mechanisms which countries currently utilize right now.

Donald Trump, among other politicians and high level individuals have accused China of currency manipulation.

With China holding trillions in dollar-denominated debt, they ultimately hold the power to crush the U.S. in their hands.

Economic sanctions tighten the noose around the neck of countless countries, as their citizens struggle for life, then begin upheaval and civil unrest before the light begins to fade.

Biological War

Countless laboratories in major cities admittedly create deadly strains of viruses for "research".

According to Richard Ebright, a biosafety expert at Rutgers University, "More than 200 incidents of loss or release of bioweapons agents from U.S. laboratories are reported each year."

In a September 2000 document written by PNAC (Dick Cheney, Donald Rumsfeld, and Jeb Bush), it discussed the introduction of a "race-specific bio-weapon" to be deployed if needed.

Cyber War

NSA whistleblower, Edward Snowden, leaked millions of documents which exposed how impressively abundant and invasive the data collection of the U.S. government truly is.

Every single piece of data is tracked, recorded, documented, and analyzed to later be data mined should the government require any "useful" information.

With increasing frequency, many high level government websites and personnel have been hacked, and various groups/individuals have claimed responsibility.

Just think about the possible implications of a cyber war when the stock exchanges, banking and investment services, government resources, top secret data, and practically everything imaginable is in some way connected and dependent on the internet.

All possible from anywhere in the world with a touch of a button.

Information War

Endless possibilities exist for war, whether it appears on a battlefield across the world, or through digital means in the blink of an eye.

Understand that the prime objective of the globalists is divide and rule.

Everyone is just a player in a game which distracts us, holds us back from gaining knowledge, and attempts to categorize and manipulate us with propaganda.

Do not be a pawn.

Section 4
Action Steps

Financial Education

Where are your savings right now?

The strategy for the general public is to "invest for the long term in a well-diversified portfolio".

To those in the finance industry, they would suggest: Mutual funds, cash, retirement accounts, and for the riskier investor, stocks.

Nothing but paper.

Un-Educated

With patience and precision, the Rockefeller's and Carnegie's have molded and shaped our education system to create a workforce of obedient minions.

Billions of dollars have been spent in the U.S. alone on different programs such as No Child Left Behind.

Just as we can't rely on the banksters to manage our money, we can't rely on the education system to be our only source of knowledge.

Warning

When the world stops using the U.S. dollar and this collapse takes full effect, unemployment will skyrocket and your local banker will be the next food stamp recipient.

Certainly you've noticed that any negative news about the economy gets pushed into the fringe category next to the news about the most recent Sasquatch and Loch Ness Monster citing.

The truth is that in 1929, right before the Great Depression occurred, it was declared that the market was now in a state of perpetual growth which would never cease.

In 2007, economic "experts" claimed that housing would always go up in value without exception.

How foolish.

Get Real

We must protect ourselves and it's quite evident that we can't rely on our government, our financial advisors, and the mainstream media.

Maximum diversity is essential in this time, possibly more than ever in history.

The first order of business is to find a place for your savings and that doesn't mean in a bank.

Investment Options

Are your savings really safe?

Unfortunately, financial education is never taught in schools so we are forced to rely on the banks to make those choices for us.

So where should you put your money?

False Choices

Your financial advisor will suggest that there are five main options: Mutual funds, stocks, bonds, retirement accounts, or banks accounts.

All of these options are gambling and should be considered dangerous choices for the foreseeable future.

Let's go over a brief rundown of why all of these are doomed to fail.

Stocks

They are a great way to make money if you are on the inside of the deal.

If your name is Warren Buffett, you'll know in advance of market crashes. Otherwise, you'll just be a statistic like many of the other fools from the Dot Com boom and bust.

Mutual Funds

Tied directly to the stock market with one extra disadvantage: You aren't even in control of the stocks you indirectly own.

You get all of the risks of stocks without the safety net of being able to put a sell order in advance.

Bonds

With cities and countries going bankrupt, a bond based on their debt is flushing your savings down the toilet.

Surely not all countries will default on their loans. However, they will be widespread and average citizens holding bonds will never see their money again.

As bail-in's become more prevalent, bondholders could

face losses while bank failures persist.

In addition, negative interest rates have made their way into the fixed-income category and trillions of dollars of bonds sell at a negative rate. That's a guaranteed loss.

Retirement Accounts

Advertisements bombard the public to invest in retirement accounts to provide them with income once they retire.

Again, these are tied to the stock market which is extremely volatile. Not to mention the threat of them being hijacked by the government as was done with pension funds in countries such as Portugal.

Bank Accounts

The choice for those not looking to take any risk.

However, bank accounts are now up for grabs because in 2013, in Cyprus, the government implemented a bail-in strategy and took money right out of citizens accounts!

In Canada, the 2013 and 2016 budget reports proposed the use of a "Bail-In Regime" in the "unlikely" event that the banks need to be recapitalized.

In 2014, the G20 met in Brisbane, Australia to discuss the implementation of a global bail-in policy should banks encounter potential failure.

Tick, Tock

Time is running out as we see the sovereignty of countless nations handed over to the supranational globalists.

Avoid risk and observe with caution as the once calm waters begin to stir and swell.

Preserve Wealth And Profit

The tide is rising as this wave approaches our shores.

Everything you've worked hard for is at risk and it's all because of the greed of globalists who control our governments.

Quadrillions of derivatives have been created which sit on top of our backs, as we wait for it to snap.

If a collapse is imminent, we need to allocate our savings appropriately or we will sink to the bottom of the ocean.

Get Real

There are many choices but there is one constant: Real assets.

A dollar is only worth the paper it's printed on.

This is broken down in great detail in *The Money GPS* but let's briefly go over why these assets are attractive.

Precious Metals

Central banks around the world have been buying more gold over the years, slowly diversifying out of the U.S. dollar.

China and India each consumed over 1000 tonnes of gold in a single year, creating massive demand on the miners, minters, and distributors.

Jewelry

While jewelry doesn't have a melt value as high as bullion, it does provide a method of holding value over long periods of time, where families can pass wealth down.

It's good for the non-savvy investor because they can get something they enjoy but won't depreciate like a liability for example.

Real Estate

There are four ways to earn income with real estate: Appreciation, depreciation, tax incentives, and cash flow.

In a worst case scenario, you'll always have a place to live.

Property

A house or condo aren't the only options for those wanting to own property.

Think smaller! Renting out a parking spot or storage locker in a good area could be very profitable, be less of a headache, and of course, require less capital.

These could be located in a condo building, but are also available all around your city. Check classified ad websites.

Land and farmland could be an excellent place to keep your wealth and eventually could be divided up into separate lots and sold separately.

Collectibles

For those who know what they're doing, collectibles are an interesting way to keep your wealth.

Numismatic coins for example could earn multiples more than bullion in a bull market but come at a premium to purchase.

Storable Food

Our most essential asset is one that is most overlooked. Storable food purchased now offers you the peace of mind that your family will be able to eat after the 72 hours it takes to empty the store shelves.

In a hyperinflationary scenario, food may become too expensive to buy, so having it tucked away may be a life saver.

Bank Holiday

There will be a bank holiday, leaving you without access to your savings. A crime that has occurred countless times throughout history.

If your wealth is in these establishments, you will kneel at the feet of your government and beg for resolution.

If you're outside the banking institutions (No paper assets, debt, loans), you will be strong while the general population suffers.

Every minute your savings sit in the bank, the tide continues to rise, threatening everything you have.

Financial Freedom

Money is simply a means to an end. We need it for our daily expenses: Food, electricity, and other bills.

The truth is that the monetary system is entirely manipulated by the globalists and it doesn't seem to be leaving their hands anytime soon.

In an effort to counteract this deception, I present you with: *The Money GPS Strategy*.

The goal: To reduce an individual's dependence on the economic system in order to attain maximum safety, security, and self-reliance.

This monetary system is designed to keep you in poverty consciousness, always struggling to make ends meet.

Run Or Hide?

Investors have decided to take a risk and pour their savings into the stock market, hoping that it will rise.

The stock market can make gains for eternity, however, historically the paper dollars that it's traded in have been devalued in relation to real goods such as food.

Paper assets are extremely risky since the Financial Crisis and it's better to follow *The Money GPS Strategy* to maintain the highest level of security.

How To Remain Safe

The majority of financial advisors will only discuss paper assets, while more perceptive individuals will claim their diversification by purchasing precious metals.

The Money GPS explores every avenue of security for your wealth because quite frankly, this could be life and death for some people.

The consensus with most financial planners is that you need to consistently make more money because the cost of living increases as time goes on.

In addition to this, they will consistently promote giving up a percentage of your savings into a retirement account which locks you in until 65 years of age with the intention of having income when you retire.

The Money GPS Strategy shatters this false paradigm, yet is more secure and simple than any other strategy generally encountered.

The Strategy

To put it succinctly, instead of working yourself to the bone to increase your income to pay your debt and bills, eliminate as much of them as possible and live the same lifestyle with less fiat currency.

When you can reduce your expenditures to a small amount, you are greatly protected from disaster far beyond any traditional asset.

The Money GPS Strategy

The Money GPS Strategy allows those who employ it, the ability to minimize their dependence on this failed and manipulated economic system.

The following is a brief breakdown of each section within *The Money GPS Strategy*.

Debt

First and foremost, criminal financial institutions have swindled politicians into creating a system which is no longer based on real wealth but instead on debt.

Since this structure is built around debt, as we become more in debt, we actually support and fuel the bankers.

You can escape this prison created by the bankers by

paying off all debt, including mortgages, regardless of the interest rates.

Savings

Remove your savings from the bank and purchase real assets and take action on strategies like those discussed in this chapter to increase security and safety.

Banks are heavily indebted, controlling trillions in derivatives just waiting to implode, these banks are implementing negative interest rates, and there is also the threat of bail-in's which will invariably occur worldwide.

Since banks have countless opportunities for risk, put your hard earned savings into something which would allow you to be free of this system altogether.

Solar Panels

As energy prices continue to rise, we need to offset this and perhaps the best way is to use solar power.

For a portion of the amount many savers have in their retirement accounts, you could power your entire house with solar. This is far greater security than a 401k/RRSP.

Many governments around the world offer a subsidy or tax rebate program as an incentive for solar panels so it is essential to research this for your particular area. This is a highly overlooked piece of the economic security puzzle.

Energy

Reduce the amount you pay on electricity or the usage of your solar panel system by switching your light bulbs to LED. Additionally, LED bulbs last a considerable amount of time which will save you money over the long term.

Sealing air leaks, making your windows more efficient, properly insulating your home, getting a programmable thermostat, and using a power strip/surge protector to turn off devices which are not in use will compound and ultimately significantly reduce your long-term energy costs.

Food

As food prices rise, individuals will find the share of their income increasingly going towards the purchase of food.

To offset this, growing a garden is the simplest strategy to not only get better quality food, but to have your own for free.

For those living in a home without land such as an apartment, sprouts and herbs can be grown indoors for pennies.

Preparation

In a crisis of any sort, food will be either in shortage or in a hyperinflationary scenario, too expensive to afford.

Buying a small supply of storable/non-perishable food now will be the best insurance policy you could ever have.

Water

Water is an essential component for survival and suddenly what we take for granted could be difficult to get.

It has been said that future wars will be fought over water.

A rainwater collection system is the best way to take control of your indispensable need of this priceless resource.

Real spring water can be the healthiest and purest source of water and best of all, it's free. For a great resource, look into findaspring.com.

Digging a well would include upfront costs but it allows you to control your own supply of water right on your own property.

A high quality water filter such as a Berkey will allow you to take the worst quality water and turn it into excellent drinking water. The filters will last 5-10 years and best of all, it requires no power.

More Strategies

- Sell items you have and don't need.

- Call all of your service providers and ask to renegotiate a better deal (Internet, phone, insurance).
- Advertise your services on classified ad websites as well as public message boards in your city.

Uncertain Future

Now consider if you implemented these simple strategies, how much money your monthly expenses would decrease by.

There is a direct proportional relationship with the level of self-sufficiency and the level of personal security you experience, particularly as conditions continue to worsen.

The Money GPS Strategy is a guaranteed formula to break free of this system of economic slavery.

How To Fight Back

In a strategic plan to separate humanity and prevent our unity, the globalists, along with assistance from the mainstream media, have brainwashed the public.

You can see this working successfully as the general public fights against their neighbour for the smallest difference without any comprehension or thought.

Divide And Conquer

This is a classic strategy known as Divide et Impera which is Latin for Divide and Rule. A strategy used for thousands of years, recorded in the pages of history.

This allows the ruling class to push people apart from one another so that they cannot unify and collectively evaporate tyranny.

People invariably occupy their minds with these planted beliefs, unknowingly victims of the master plan.

The public is distracted by the prevalence of propaganda, allowing those in control an opportunity to manipulate them.

Succeed Or Fail

We must have ammunition to destroy the globalists. The ammunition comes in the form of both information and the choices we make.

We'll fight in the information war.

It is an absolute fact that information is far more powerful than any military on earth.

To paraphrase Victor Hugo: You can't stop an idea whose time has come.

Solutions

Understand that not all of these need to be implemented for you specifically.

These are just some ideas you can use in order to peacefully push back against a tyrannical government which uses your tax dollars to keep you bound into slavery.

As we acquiesce to the globalists, we give power to this

system but opting out of it will strip their power away, slowly but surely.

First and foremost, take your savings out of the banks and put it into real assets. Once again, your money is used to fuel the banksters and their grip on the future of your savings.

Pay in cash whenever possible. Each digital transaction is tracked, added to a database, and expands the cashless society—one of the goals of the technocratic elite.

Shop at local stores and buy local products as often as possible. This punishes the globalists and their plans to weaken the economy and offshore your job.

Minimize your dependence on the power grid by investing in solar power for your home which will protect you in a hyperinflation or natural disaster.

Put a dagger into biotech companies who are destroying the food supply, by never buying foods that contain genetically modified organisms, such as processed food.

Put down the TV remote and pick up a book. This will expand your mind while simultaneously preventing their propaganda from attacking you.

Protect your family by securing your home with as many lines of defence as you can afford.

Use your freedom of speech to speak up against oppression, tyranny, and the advancement of the globalist agenda.

Debt Slaves

There are countless ways to fight back against the system that enslaves us and we need to begin today.

If you stop complying and begin changes to your lifestyle and the choices you make, you will weaken their power while simultaneously being sheltered from the crisis.

Always remember that we are the frontline infantry in this battle against globalist rule.

Brace yourselves for an uncertain future.

Made in the USA
San Bernardino, CA
10 March 2018